Genius at Work! GREAT INVENTOR BIOGRAPHIES

# The Guy Who Invented Home Video Games

## Ralph Baer and His Awesome Invention

Edwin Brit Wyckoff

**Enslow Elementary**
an imprint of
**Enslow Publishers, Inc.**
40 Industrial Road
Box 398
Berkeley Heights, NJ 07922
USA
http://www.enslow.com

*Many thanks to Ralph Baer for sharing his time and memories during multiple interviews with the author and his generous willingness to provide photos.*

**Series Literary Consultant**
Allan A. De Fina, PhD
Dean, College of Education and Professor of Literacy Education
New Jersey City University
Past President of the New Jersey Reading Association



Enslow Elementary, an imprint of Enslow Publishers, Inc.

Enslow Elementary® is a registered trademark of Enslow Publishers, Inc.



**Library of Congress Cataloging-in-Publication Data**

Wyckoff, Edwin Brit.
The guy who invented home video games : Ralph Baer and his awesome invention / Edwin Brit Wyckoff.
p. cm. — (Genius at work!)
Includes bibliographical references and index.
Summary: "Read about Ralph Baer and find out how he invented the first video games"—Provided by publisher.
ISBN 978-0-7660-3450-1
1. Baer, Ralph H.—Juvenile literature. 2. Video games—United States—History—Juvenile literature. 3. Video games industry—United States—History—Juvenile literature. 4. Inventors—United States—Biography—Juvenile literature. 5. Engineers—United States—Biography—Juvenile literature. I. Title.
GV1469.3.W93 2011
794.8—dc22
2009042815

Printed in the United States of America

102011 Lake Book Manufacturing, Inc., Melrose Park, IL

10 9 8 7 6 5 4 3 2



**Photo Credits:** Archives Center, National Museum of American History, Smithsonian Institution, pp. 1 (upper left), 19; Artville, p. 8; Associated Press, p. 25; courtesy of Ralph Baer, pp. 1 (lower right), 6, 14, 15, 20, 21, 26, 29; Everett Collection, pp. 17, 22; Photos.com, pp. 13, 28; Shutterstock, pp. 3, 5; United States Holocaust Memorial Museum, courtesy of Bob Reed, p. 10.

**Cover Photos:** Front cover—Shutterstock (background); courtesy of Ralph Baer (inset); back cover—Shutterstock.

# Contents

Chapter 1

# The Battle Zone

The young boy sat staring into a black tunnel. Scary growling sounds came out of the darkness. His heart thumped inside his chest as ghostlike soldiers raced toward him. Terrified, he squeezed the triggers in his hands and blasted one wild ghost after another without stopping them. The roars grew louder and louder until one voice wiped out all the others. "Come to dinner, honey, everything is getting cold." He blasted one more ghost, then turned off the video game and walked toward his mother in the dining room with his heart still thumping.

Two blocks away, a seventy-two-year-old lady was swinging, swaying, and smashing tennis balls over the net on her TV screen. There was no tennis

All kinds of people enjoy playing video games.

Ralph Baer, surrounded by some of the games he invented.

racket in sight, just an electronic controller in her hand and a smile of victory on her face.

Later that night, a man switched off the last news report. Gripping the wheel of a power-hungry racing car, he roared into first place on his child's video game. Upstairs, the family slept quietly while he zoomed his car around the track.

All around the world, millions of video consoles and games are alive with action. Millions of them bring in billions of dollars in sales every year. But a few years ago there was nothing: no Xbox, no Guitar Hero, no PlayStation, no Wii.

Way back in 1968, a TV engineer in Manchester, New Hampshire, built the first home video game console. He figured out how to send electronic messages to TV sets. And he designed the first home video games. Not enough people know his name.

Chapter 2

# The Invisible Boy

Rudolf Heinrich Baer was born March 8, 1922, in the little German town of Pirmasens. His folks called him Rolf. His father, Leo, worked as a traveling salesman for a local shoe factory. His mother, Lotte, stayed home with him and his younger sister, Ilse. The people of Germany were living through terrible times. Their money was worth so little it took a whole suitcase full of cash to buy a loaf of bread.

In 1929, when Rolf was only seven years old, factories shut down and jobs disappeared. This awful time spread throughout the world and was called the Great Depression. There was almost no money anywhere. By 1932, scared and angry German citizens began to support the Nazi Party. Their leader, Adolf Hitler, screamed hate-filled speeches on the radio. He blamed the Jews for Germany's problems. Listeners would sit by their radios, hearing one hundred thousand voices shouting "Heil Hitler! Heil Hitler!" over and over again. In their minds' eyes, they could see one hundred thousand arms shoot forward in the Nazi salute.

In 1937, Rolf's father wrote to his American cousins, asking them if they would take in his family if they could get to the United States. They wrote back, saying, "Yes, come to us. Stay with us." Getting passports to leave Germany was not easy. The Nazis controlled everything.

Hitler Youth members in a stadium

Rolf remembers being thrown out of school because he was Jewish. He will never forget the last day he spoke to an old schoolmate who bicycled past wearing a Nazi Youth uniform. The boys said just a few words. After that, none of his friends ever talked to Rolf again. Boys who had grown up with him came up and almost walked through him. It was as if he were invisible.

Finally, the Baer family escaped to Holland. Carrying precious passports to America, they sailed on the ocean liner *Nieuw Amsterdam* in August 1938.

Less than three months later, the Nazis broke into thousands of Jewish stores in Germany and Austria. They smashed the windows. They burned Jewish synagogues. The violent nightmare of the Holocaust was beginning.

Chapter 3

# Made in America

The Baer family landed in New York Harbor in the middle of a heat wave so extreme that Rolf thought they were in Africa. Cousins and uncles and aunts crowded around and took them into their homes. The Baers started their American adventure by changing Rolf's name to Ralph and Ilse's name to Jane. Sixteen-year-old Ralph went to work in a factory owned by someone in the family. Riding to work in the subway, he caught sight of an ad in another rider's magazine: "Make Big Money in Radio and Television Servicing."

Ralph spent $1.25 a week from his twelve-dollar salary for the correspondence course at the National Radio Institute. He graduated in 1940, then plunged into repairing, building, and rebuilding radios.

A radio of the 1930s or 1940s. People who could repair radios were in great demand, especially after World War II started.

On December 7, 1941, Japanese planes attacked Pearl Harbor in Hawaii, destroying many U.S. navy ships. America went to war. It was almost impossible to buy new things—especially radios. Nineteen-year-old Ralph raced from job to job in radio repair shops all over New York City. And then he sat up nights teaching himself math and history. He was drafted into the army in 1943, sworn in as a citizen of the United States of America, and shipped off. He was twenty-one and headed right back to Europe, now torn by war.

Baer teamed up with a couple of dozen other German-speaking soldiers and sold the U.S. Army on a very smart idea. They could teach American soldiers how to spot enemy equipment and how to destroy it. They showed three hundred thousand soldiers how German tanks and guns worked. Baer was a ferocious collector, spotting and carting off eighteen tons of enemy war equipment. Then he got the army to haul it to the United States and set it up in training camps.

Baer in his Army uniform

The war ended in 1945, when Baer was only twenty-three years old. He had a choice to make: He could go back to New York City to work on radios. Or he could go back to school to learn all about TV.

Ralph Baer always wanted to go forward rather than backward. He decided to go to college in Chicago. He graduated from the American Television Institute of Technology in 1949, then moved to New York to start his career.

He married Dena Whinston in 1952. They had three children—James, Mark, and Nancy. Eventually,

The Baer family: Nancy, Ralph, James, Mark (in back), and Dena

James followed his father into engineering. Mark, a lawyer, became an assistant attorney general in Salt Lake City, Utah. Nancy became an artist. Their dad kept moving up from one job to a better one in the high-tech world of military electronics. He landed at Sanders Associates in Manchester, New Hampshire. There he was in charge of a staff of five hundred designers and engineers.

One bright day in August 1966, Baer had an amazing, exciting idea. He was waiting for one of his engineers at the bus station in New York City. Baer was early. He sat down in the sun thinking about television and letting his mind wander and wonder.

Chapter 4

# "What Else Can a TV Do?"

The question of what else a TV could do really bothered Ralph Baer. After all, television was a magical box. There were more than 50 million TV sets in the United States. But everybody just sat staring at all that expensive equipment. Baer wondered whether TV sets could play games with us.

An ad for television sets from 1950

Some questions take years to answer. But Baer's idea turned into reality fairly quickly. He pulled a small spiral notebook out of his pocket, put it on his knee, and drew a quick technical diagram. Then he started scribbling the names of games.

Almost shouting to himself, he rapped out a list: football, hockey, Ping-Pong, volleyball, handball, soccer. In his imagination, he chased little cartoon characters through mazes and powered racing cars up and down hills and valleys. When the other engineer showed up, Baer snapped the notebook shut and climbed aboard the bus.

Baer asked Sanders Associates for money to develop a video game console—a machine that would allow people to play games with their TV sets. His boss said, "Forget it! Stop playing games." Secretly Baer built a very simple game box. An executive at Sanders got him a budget of twenty-five hundred dollars, saying "This looks like it has potential, but it better do more interesting things." Baer bought a cheap plastic toy gun, hooked it into the box, and kept working. Sanders gave him a little more money for

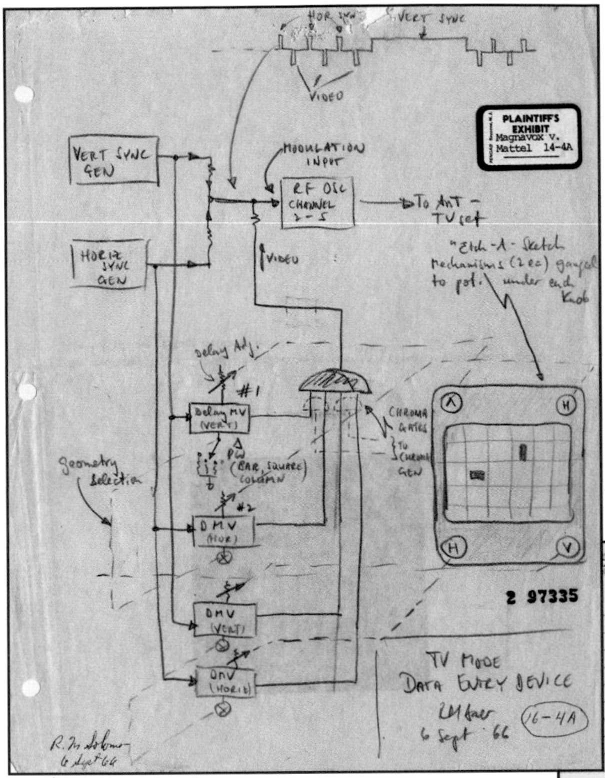

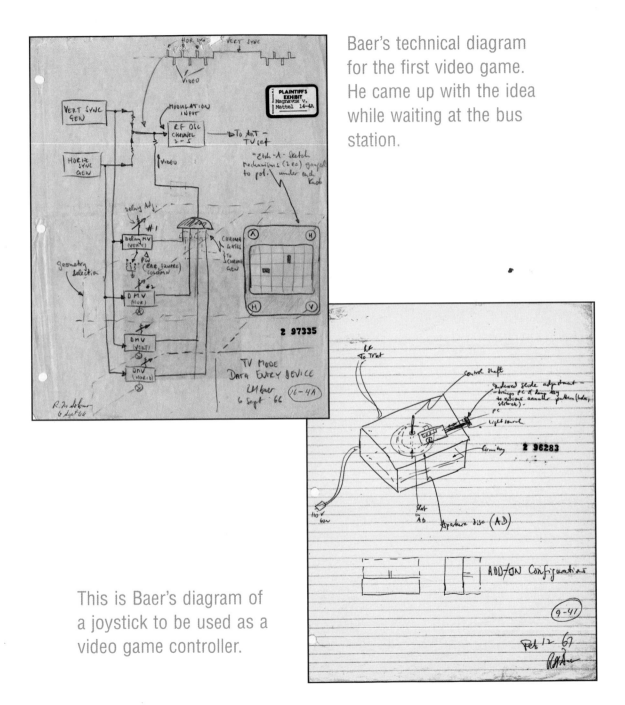

Baer's technical diagram for the first video game. He came up with the idea while waiting at the bus station.

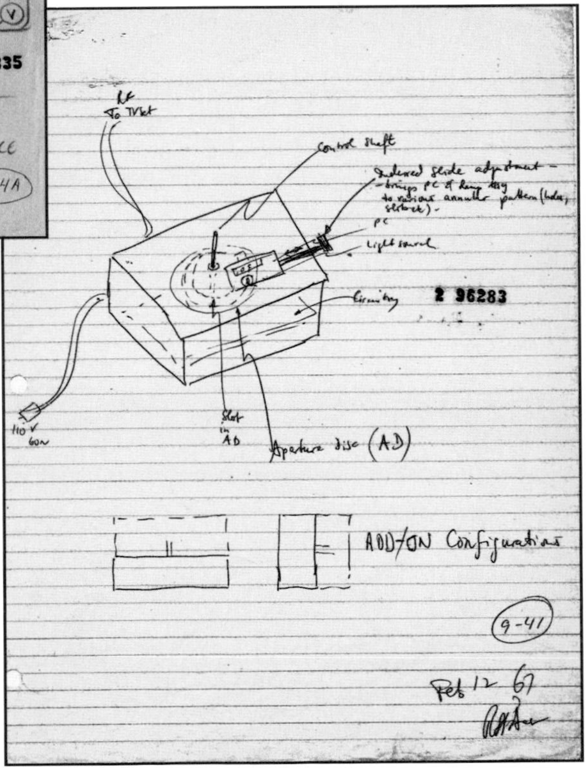


This is Baer's diagram of a joystick to be used as a video game controller.

The Brown Box, the first video game console, was used with a toy gun.

the project, and by 1968, Baer had a console neatly covered with brown wood-grain paper. It was stuffed with three hundred parts and could run several simple games. The research director laughed. “It won’t sell,” he said, “but I guess you’ve got to play.”

Baer and his technician, Bill Harrison, who had built those early game systems, nicknamed the console the Brown Box. They showed it to leading television manufacturers. There were no takers. A bored executive asked Baer, "Are you still fooling around with that stuff?" Finally, in 1970, Magnavox, a leading TV set manufacturer, offered to pay Baer royalties—an amount of money for permission to

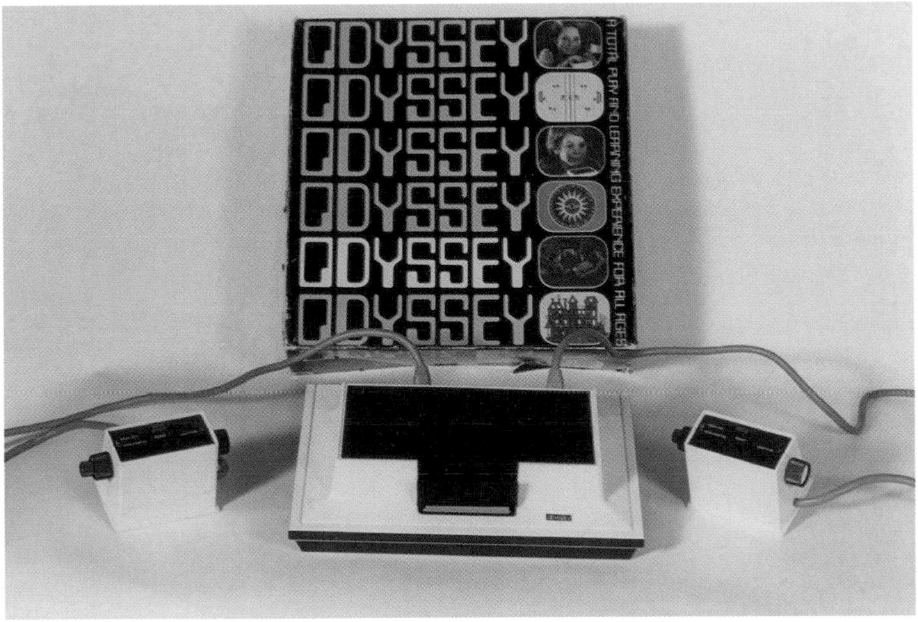


The Magnavox company was licensed to sell Baer's invention. They named it the Odyssey.

Video game consoles are actually highly specialized computers. All video game systems contain the following parts:

- A device that allows the player to play the game, such as a controller, joystick, or steering wheel (known as the user control interface)
- A central processing unit (CPU), like that in a computer
- Random access memory (RAM), which stores games as they are being played
- Software that allows different parts of the system to communicate with each other
- Storage medium (such as a CD or memory card)
- Video and audio output connected to the TV
- Power supply

When Ralph Baer developed the first video game console, microprocessors had not even been invented. The Odyssey put out by Magnavox used transistors. Its graphics were very simple. To play it, you had to tape a plastic overlay on the front of the television set.

An ad for the Odyssey system

(Adapted from Jeff Tyson, "How Videogame Systems Work," HowStuffWorks.com, October 16, 2000, <http://electronics.howstuffworks.com/video-game.htm> [October 7, 2009].)

develop and market Baer's game ideas. They took over the Brown Box, and Baer went back to designing military equipment.

For Baer, the excitement was over. All the extra work at night had worn him down physically. It was a low period for a man always running on high. He was lying in a hospital bed waiting for an operation when three of his coworkers ran in cheering and carrying a giant bank check three feet wide. Baer sat up to read the amount: one hundred thousand dollars! More royalty checks followed as Magnavox sold 350,000 Odyssey home video games—based on Ralph Baer's breakthrough technology.

## Chapter 5

# Honors and Surprises

Very often, losers have lonely lives, but winners always seem to discover crowds of friends in their corner. Everybody seemed to remember how they had encouraged Baer and supported his ideas. His next winning invention was a game console called Simon. It had color and sound. It is still selling. And Ralph H. Baer is still inventing, advising game developers, meeting with industry leaders around the world, and picking up awards.

On February 13, 2006, President George W. Bush invited Baer to the White House and gave him the National Medal of Technology for being "the father of home video games." The Japanese and Brazilian governments gave him their highest awards for technology.

In 2006, President George W. Bush gave the National Medal of Technology to Ralph Baer.

An unexpected surprise came when a law school in New Hampshire gave him an honorary law degree. Baer is not a lawyer, but he had to defend his inventions in court for sixteen years. Several companies tried to use his inventions without paying any royalties. Baer fought for his rights, and he learned how to use the law to defend his ideas. He won the legal battle every time.

Video game systems have grown into a $28 billion industry worldwide. Production budgets are as big as budgets for blockbuster movies—$80 to $100 million each. Thousands of people design and build games and game systems. Universities offer degrees in game design. David Bowie and other famous musicians work on games. George Lucas, who created

# Some of Ralph Baer's Amazing Inventions

Genius at Work!

- First light-gun games (1967–1968)
- ODYSSEY game system (1971–1972)
- Pioneered interactive video game (1975)
- KID-VID, a preschool game featuring music, and SIMON, a hand-held game with music and color (1978–1979)

- MANIAC hand-held games (1979–1981)
- LASER COMMAND electro-optical toy (1985)

- SMARTY BEAR VIDEO, an interactive toy in a teddy bear (1987)

- SOUNDS-BY-ME, an interactive book (1994)
- BIKE MAX (1996)
- TALKING TOOLS (2000)

(From Sanders Associates: "Once Upon A Time The Video Game ..." <www.pong-story.com/sanders.htm>)

the *Star Wars* movies, loves designing video games. Producers such as Jerry Bruckheimer turn their movie hits into exciting home video games.

The engineer with the little notebook asked himself one big question, "What else can a television set do?" The answer is endless. It changes our world—turns it from flat to three-dimensional; turns us into music makers; turns us into athletes who race around the room smacking an electronic ball into a wild and wonderful future.

Ralph H. Baer, now in his late eighties, is still out front working on that future.

**1922** Born March 8 to Leo and Lotte Baer in Pirmasens, Germany.

**1936** Thrown out of school for being Jewish.

**1938** Sails to New York City aboard the *Nieuw Amsterdam.* Name changed from Rudolph (Rolf) to Ralph H. Baer.

**1940** Studies radio repair at National Radio Institute.

**1943** Drafted into U.S. Army. Becomes citizen. Goes to war in Europe.

**1946** Leaves Army to study TV engineering at the American Television Institute of Technology in Chicago.

**1949** Graduates as engineer. Returns to New York.

**1952** Marries Dena Whinston; they have two boys and one girl.

**1966** Becomes manager of equipment design at Sanders Associates in Manchester, New

Hampshire. While waiting at bus stop, sketches home video console.

1968 Builds "Brown Box" video game console.

1972 Magnavox licenses Baer's patent. Pays royalties.

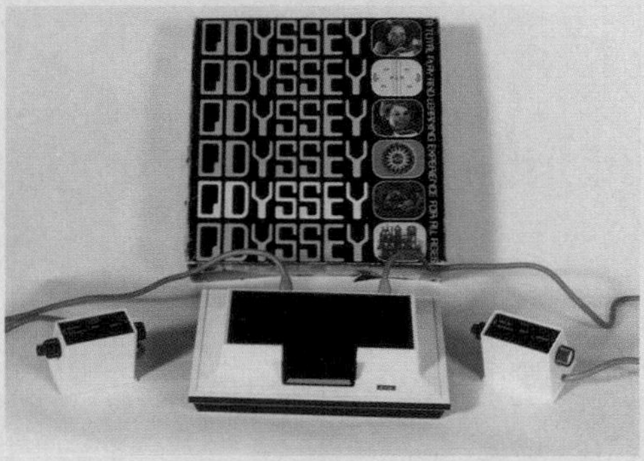


2006 Receives National Medal of Technology from President George W. Bush, who calls him "the father of home video games."

# Words to Know

**budget**—An amount of money that can be used for a project.

**console**—A box containing electronics that produce video game signals

**engineer**—Someone who is trained to use scientific knowledge to build things.

**executive**—An officer or manager of a business.

**Nazis (NOT-zees)**—Members of a German political party led by Adolf Hitler, in power from 1933 to 1945.

**potential**—Having more power or value than can be seen now.

**royalty**—A payment for using someone else's property or ideas.

## Books

Baer, Ralph H. *Videogames: In the Beginning.* Springfield, N.J.: Rolenta Press, 2005.

Cunningham, Kevin. *Video Game Designer.* Ann Arbor, Mich: Cherry Lake Publishing, 2009.

Parker, Janice. *Machines: Science Q & A.* New York: Weigl Publishers, 2008.

Platt, Richard. *Eureka! Great Inventions and How They Happened.* Boston: Kingfisher, 2003.

## Internet Addresses

Genesis: How the Home Video Games Industry Began
<www.ralphbaer.com/how_video_games.htm>

How Stuff Works: How Videogame Systems Work
<http://electronics.howstuffworks.com/video-game.htm>

Sanders Associates: "Once Upon A Time The Video Game . . ."
<www.pong-story.com/sanders.htm>

# Index